Top Notes

John Misto's

The Shoe-Horn Sonata

Study notes for Standard English:
Module A
2015-2020 HSC

Bruce Pattinson

A
FIVE SENSES
PUBLICATION

Five Senses Education Pty Ltd
2/195 Prospect Highway
Seven Hills 2147
New South Wales
Australia

Pattinson, Bruce,
Top Notes – Shoe-horn Sonata
ISBN 978 -1- 76032- 031 - 7

CONTENTS

INTRODUCTION TO THE TOP NOTES SERIES

Top Notes are designed with the high school student in mind. They are written in an easy to read manner yet discuss the important ideas and issues that need to be understood in order to successfully undertake English HSC examinations.

Top Notes are written by practising teachers who have years of experience. These guides contain many helpful tips for the course and examination. They focus specifically on student needs and examine each text in the context of the module and elective to which it has been allocated.

Each text includes:

- Notes on the specific module
- Plot summary
- Character analysis
- Setting
- Thematic concerns
- Language studies
- Essay questions and response
- Other textual material
- Practice questions
- Useful quotes

I am sure you will find these Top Notes useful in your study of English.

Bruce Pattinson
Series Editor

THE STANDARD COURSE

This is a brief analysis of the Standard course to ensure you are completely familiar with what you are attempting in the examination. If in any doubt at all check with your teacher or the Board of Studies.

The Standard Course requires you to have studied:

- Four prescribed texts. This means four texts from the list given to your teacher by the Board of Studies.

- For each of the texts, one must come from each of the following four categories.
  - drama
  - poetry
  - prose fiction (novel usually)
  - nonfiction or media or film or multimedia texts. (Multimedia are CD ROMs, websites, etc.)

- A range of related texts of your own choosing. These are part of your Area of Study, Module A and Module C. Do not confuse these with the main set text you are studying.

Paper One

Area of Study: Discovery

Paper Two

Module A	*Module B*	*Module C*
Experience through Language	**Close Study of Text**	**Texts and Society**
Electives	▪ Drama	*Electives*
▪ Distinctive Voices	OR	▪ Exploring Interactions
OR	▪ Prose Fiction	OR
▪ Distinctively Visual	OR	▪ Exploring Transitions
	▪ Nonfiction, Film, Media, Multimedia	
	OR	
	▪ Poetry	

You must study the Area of Study and EACH of Modules A, B and C

There are options within EACH of these that your school will select.

EXPERIENCE THROUGH LANGUAGE

ELECTIVE TWO: Distinctively Visual

The Experience through Language module demands language be the focus of study and therefore, your response. The syllabus requires a focus on how language can shape relationships and change perceptions of other people and the world. The Board says about this Module,

'This module requires students to explore the uses of a particular aspect of language. **It develops students' awareness of language and helps them understand how our perceptions of and relationships with others and the world are shaped in written, spoken and visual language'** (p.11).

You will be studying a specific text, in this case the play, *The Shoe-Horn Sonata* by John Misto. In your responses, you should always be discussing how language has been used as a technique by the composer. Note the three types of language specified above. In this text, it is expected to you will encounter written language in the script. In a performance of the play you encounter spoken language as well as visual language, through costuming, backdrops and mise en scene. Remember a play is best studied in performance.

The elective you will be studying in this module is called, "Distinctly Visual". BOSTES expects,

'In their responding and composing, students explore the ways the images we see and/or visuals in texts are created. Students consider how the forms, features and language of different texts create these images, affect interpretation and shape meaning. Students examine one prescribed text, in addition to other related texts of their own choosing that provide examples of the distinctively visual.' (p.12)

In other words you will be studying how the language of visual imagery is used to shape meaning or how written and spoken words create visual images. Many students are a little confused at first since they are often reading words on a page and not looking at pictures. They ask, "How can I look at the visual?" You need to see this elective as the exploration of visual images. All composers of creative texts try and encourage their audience to see images in their mind as they experience the text. For many years you have studied imagery in novels and poetry and never thought to ask for a photo! You will be exploring and analysing how composers use visual images to send messages or convey meaning to the audience. Composers send messages or emphasise certain aspects of a character, a relationship, an event or an idea through the use of visual images. Visual, narrative and poetic techniques are often employed by composers to create such images through language and art.

An example might help. Visual images are usually clear in films, posters and pictures. They may still be clear in written texts, but may not be as literally visual. For example, the composer of a graphic may have put a love heart between two people to indicate that they felt love for each other or were falling in love. Another example is in cartoons where the audience can see the heart of a character beating (often in a love heart shape) in their chest as the person they love walks by. Usually this is simply emphasising, through a visual symbol, the emotion that the composer wants you to notice. You may pick up the message that the character is in love simply by their body language facing the character, touching the other person frequently or even simply their facial expressions.

Thus, the composer has already portrayed their idea to us without the character even having to say, the word "love". Similarly, we get messages or get meaning from the descriptions of a character's body language. When they are not verbalising anything, we are still picking up meaning from actions. An actor may be saying the words, "I hate him" and we are also reading in the narrative about their body language, facial expressions and other techniques to confirm this or, perhaps, deny this if it is said sarcastically. These things emphasise the character's feelings for that person.

In this way, the messages the audience "read" through visual cues are just as important as what the actor is saying in helping us build visual images about the text. In some cases, as suggested there may be inconsistencies in what a character is actually saying and the way he/she is described as acting. This is very important for the audience to know and is consequently why it is so important that we can all read visual images and not just focus on the spoken language of a text.

Other visual aspects to a text may be thematic. This means the composer may create visual images to promote ideas. Here techniques such as imagery are very useful. A composer might use a technique like symbolism to help represent a message they would like the audience to think about. Other composers might add more meaning to a particular object by having it take on a symbolic significance. (For example, a motif – is a reoccurring symbol and may convey meaning due to an added significance, linked to its connotation.)

Now that you are more advanced in your study of English, the techniques are a little subtler. As you should already know, the visual images we get from description 'talk' to us and give us messages as discussed above. It is your job to explore what the main messages are in a text and then investigate how the artistic and linguistic cues present visual images which convey messages.

Visual aspects used to give the audience clues about that character and which are often seen in visual texts such as films, include the clothing (costume), the style (hair and makeup), the setting and the way all of these things have been put together, the mise en scene. All indicate something about the character. A messy bedroom will emphasise to the audience that this character is in a chaotic time in their life or that they are a lazy person who is not interested in looking after themselves. These aspects can be conveyed through a lens or through another artistic medium or through words.

When you consider how relationships are represented you will find that the composer can use many techniques to show how people interact. The types of imagery used are always carefully chosen. An uneasy relationship may be associated with unpleasant or violent images or symbols.

The ideas of a text are considered very important and these are often emphasised through distinctive images. If a writer wanted to celebrate a particular place you would expect the images created to be positive. Perhaps the images are vibrant and exciting, full of bright colours and attractive images and people. You job would be to examine how the visual images have been crafted to represent the composer's ideas (to make meaning). It is also important you consider how different composers do this in different ways. Be ready to compare and contrast. It is important to see how effective composers have been. This is why you will also be asked to gather related texts that you choose yourself. This elective requires you to become an expert on how a variety of composers such as authors, poets, film directors and artists create and use the distinctively visual. You are urged to revise the language of imagery as well as the language and vocabulary of visual literacy. Revise aspects such as colour palette, salience, vectors, gazes and reading path as they can all convey messages. Techniques will be an important aspect of this module titled, Experience through Language and of this elective, titled Distinctively Visual.

RELATED TEXTS

This module expects you to look at other texts and see how the distinctively visual has been used by composers to shape meaning. You will probably chose to gather some related texts that are essentially 'viewed.' Think for instance about film, paintings, photographs and many advertisements. It is a good idea to explore differing text types as it is important you show that you understand a range of texts create visual images in different ways. You have been studying images in your junior years and should be familiar with many common terms associated with visual literacy. Some were listed at the end of the previous page. These techniques will be very useful when you come to discuss a visual related text. You should be familiar with words such as salience, vectors, foregrounding reading paths, perspectives, gaze, the colour palette, framing and size.

The Shoe-Horn Sonata is an Australian play that explores one element of the Second World War. In studying this unit explore the play's visual elements and examine visual aspects in light of the written language. For example, consider how the various elements combine to enhance the audience's understanding and how these distinctively visual aspects blend with the content and ideas as well as offer something extra and unique.

It is important to remember that this text is a play and you need to focus on the fact that while you are reading the play in class it is meant to be watched in a theatre. As you read the play for your studies pay attention to Misto, the playwright's stage directions. Work out why the slides and songs are placed where they are and how effective they are at that particular moment in the play. Further notes on this are found in the themes section of this study guide. You need to understand the effect of the techniques that Misto uses.

Ensure, as you are studying the play, that you are considering your first responses to the ideas within it. Think about defining moments in your life and how the decisions you made have changed your life. Reflect on your own response to the play. Consider how it has changed your understanding of how things may have been in the past and how our lives have been altered by past events. You should develop a personal response to the play. Think about how you feel about the women and what they endured. Misto also questions war and how people respond to situations of stress in their lives but, more positively, he comments on the strength of the human spirit and on the power of relationships. How might this play have helped you picture aspects of the war that a textbook may not have conveyed? What techniques were employed to help you visualise such aspects?

Suggestions for Related texts start on page 91 of this Top Notes.

STUDYING A DRAMA TEXT

The medium of any text is very important. If a text is a drama this must not be forgotten. Plays are not *read* they are *viewed*. This means you should refer to the "audience" rather than the "reader." The marker will want to know you are aware of the text as a play and that you have considered its effect in performance.

Remembering a drama text is a play also means when you are exploring *how* the composer represents his/her ideas you MUST discuss dramatic techniques. This applies to any response using a drama text, irrespective of the form of the response.

Dramatic techniques are all the devices the playwright uses to represent his or her ideas. They are the elements of a drama that are manipulated by playwrights and directors to make any drama effective on stage. You might also see them referred to as dramatic devices or theatrical techniques.

Every play uses dramatic techniques differently. Some playwrights are very specific about how they want their play performed on stage. Others, like Shakespeare, give virtually no directions. They might give detailed comments at the beginning of the play and/ or during the script. These are usually in italics and are called *stage directions*. They are never spoken but provide a guide to the director and actors about how the play is to appear and sound when performed.

Some common dramatic techniques are shown on the diagram that follows.

DRAMATIC AND VISUAL TECHNIQUES

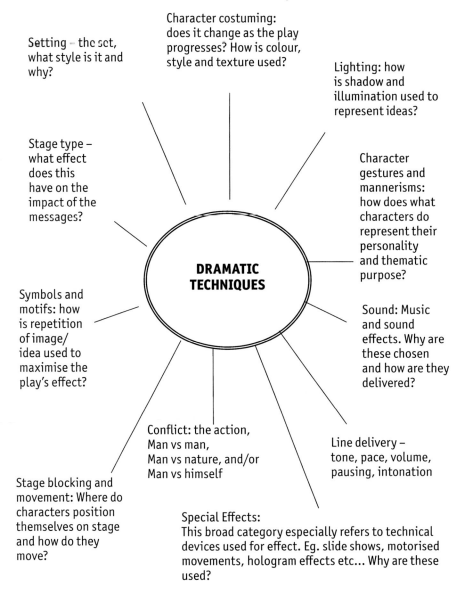

Setting – the set, what style is it and why?

Character costuming: does it change as the play progresses? How is colour, style and texture used?

Lighting: how is shadow and illumination used to represent ideas?

Stage type – what effect does this have on the impact of the messages?

Character gestures and mannerisms: how does what characters do represent their personality and thematic purpose?

DRAMATIC TECHNIQUES

Symbols and motifs: how is repetition of image/idea used to maximise the play's effect?

Sound: Music and sound effects. Why are these chosen and how are they delivered?

Conflict: the action, Man vs man, Man vs nature, and/or Man vs himself

Line delivery – tone, pace, volume, pausing, intonation

Stage blocking and movement: Where do characters position themselves on stage and how do they move?

Special Effects: This broad category especially refers to technical devices used for effect. Eg. slide shows, motorised movements, hologram effects etc... Why are these used?

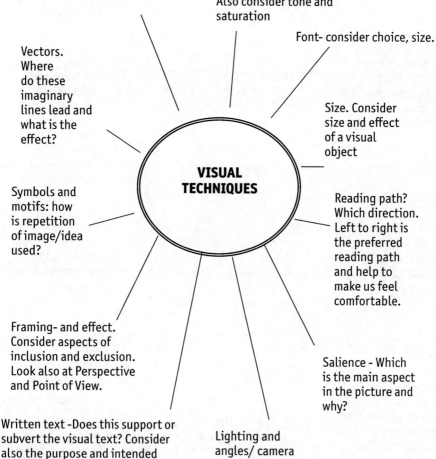

Gaze- demand or offer and effect?

Is the portrait a front on demand, or side on offer? Consider also body language and costuming.

Colour palette. Which colours are used and what do they represent? Eg White = purity, red + passion or anger. Also consider tone and saturation

Font- consider choice, size.

Vectors. Where do these imaginary lines lead and what is the effect?

Size. Consider size and effect of a visual object

VISUAL TECHNIQUES

Symbols and motifs: how is repetition of image/idea used?

Reading path? Which direction. Left to right is the preferred reading path and help to make us feel comfortable.

Framing- and effect. Consider aspects of inclusion and exclusion. Look also at Perspective and Point of View.

Salience - Which is the main aspect in the picture and why?

Written text -Does this support or subvert the visual text? Consider also the purpose and intended audience.

Lighting and angles/ camera shots. Perspectives and sense of power.

THE PLAYWRIGHT

John Misto who has been writing full time since 1981, has an extensive writing portfolio. His original training was as a lawyer. His research skills are reflected in *The Shoe-Horn Sonata*.

Some of Misto's writing credits include:

Television and Film

The Day of the Roses – The Granville Story (AFI Award 1999)

- *The Damnation of Harvey McHugh* (4 AFI Awards)
- *The Last Frontier*
- *Dirtwater Dynasty*
- *Palace of Dreams*
- *Natural Causes*
- *Peter and Pompey*
- *Survival – The Stuart Diver Story*

Plays

- *Gossamer*
- *Sky*
- *The Shoe-Horn Sonata*
- *Harp on the Willow*

The prescribed text, *The Shoe-Horn Sonata* has been performed both here and in London. It has won many awards including the NSW Premier's Literary Award (1995) and the Australia Remembers National Play Competition (1996).

John Misto currently lives in Sydney, New South Wales. As well as writing, he conducts speaking engagements for school groups.

Vera Rado, formerly known as Vera Harms, author of the introduction to John's play, accompanies the playwright when he visits schools. When just a teenager, Vera was imprisoned by the Japanese for three years under horrific conditions. John traced Vera through her letters and asked for an interview to enable him to write the play 'as honestly and accurately as possible'.

On their school visits, Vera and John talk memorably about the play's dramatic techniques and about the personal experiences of women whose lives are at the heart of *The Shoe-Horn Sonata*.

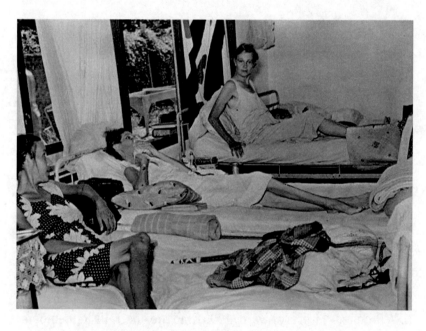

Recovering post War inmates Java, Indonesia in December 1945.
BBC News Oct 19th 2014.

CONTEXT

Background to World War Two

WWII, from 1939–1945, is considered a European war because Germany, led by Adolf Hitler, attacked all of Europe. Beginning in Czechoslovakia and moving on to Poland, Norway, Denmark, Belgium and Holland in succession, the Germans aimed to control Europe. Before long, the world was involved in the most destructive, violent and widespread war in its history.

The war in the Pacific or Far East was the result of Japanese aggression and expansionism, which had begun earlier. The Japanese invaded Manchuria in 1931 on a slight pretext and began to expand this force and take over large portions of China. They felt they needed room to expand and were also fearful of Chiang Kai-shek's Nationalist forces that were trying to unite China. When the League of Nations protested over Japanese actions they left the League in 1933 and conquered more territory in China.

Another problem was the continuing differences between the Nationalists led by Chiang Kai-shek and the Chinese Communists led by Mao who wanted to take over China. The Japanese were fiercely anti-communist and had signed a treaty with Germany and Italy to help stop communism.

In 1937 Japan invaded China and they advanced quickly. They captured Beijing and much of the eastern coast but by 1939 the war had gone into stalemate because of the size of the country and the problem of supply. Also the Nationalists had again decided to fight the communists rather than have the two fight together against the invaders. Countries such as Russia and America supplied them with weapons to help defeat the communists.

On December 7, 1941 the Japanese made a surprise attack on the Americans at Pearl Harbour and were then at war with the western allies. The Americans declared war the next day. All citizens of the allies were then at war with the Japanese and were sent to camps after being rounded up as the Japanese conquered much of South East Asia and Burma. Thousands died at the hands of Japanese brutality, especially after the initial advances they made up until 1943 began to stall all over the Pacific region.

Much has been written about the cruelty and brutality of the Japanese soldiers toward prisoners during the war. It is well documented that they were incredibly harsh on prisoners including women and children. The Japanese used prisoners as slave labour and starved many to death. The incidents described in the text are realistic, deliberately so, and relate closely to the Distinctively Visual.

Even at the end of the war in 1945 the Japanese still fought hard and the Allied advance was slow on the ground. After the two atomic bombs were dropped on the 6th and 9th of August 1945 the Japanese finally surrendered on the 14th of August. It was only after this that all the horrific cruelties they had made prisoners endure were uncovered.

The following images may assist in your understanding of the issues involved. If you are interested in photography, explore some war photographs and photographers. Explore the work of CW Bean(WWI), the so called Robert Capa or Nick Ut.

IMAGES OF WORLD WAR TWO

MUSIC AND SONG LIST

You could listen to some of these on Youtube. page numbers are taken from the Currency Press version of the play printed in 2014.

- *Fall in Brother* – marching song page 2
- *Rule Britannia* – patriotic song page 22
- *Something to Remember You By* – by Dinah Shore page 29
- *Jerusalem* – patriotic hymn page 36 and prior scene
- *Happy Times* – by Joe Stafford page 41
- *Bolero* – by Ravel page 46
- *English Country Gardens* – by Percy Granger page 47
- *O Come All Ye Faithful* – Christmas Carol page 52
- *God Rest Ye Merry Gentlemen* – Christmas Carol page 53
- *We'll Meet Again* – by the Inkspots page 53
- *Unknown Song* - page 60
- *The Captive's Hymn* – page 63
- *Unknown lyrics* – page 65
- *When You're Smiling* - by Judy Garland page 68
- *I'll Walk Alone* – by Anne Shelton page 72
- *Fur Elise, Country Garden, Humoresque, Danny Boy* – page 73
- *You'll Never Know How Much I Love You* – by Alice Faye page 75
- *Whispering Grass* – by the Inkspots page 79
- *The Blue Danube Waltz* by Johann Strauss page 82
- *Danny Boy* – performed by Glenn Miller's Orchestra page 83
- *An Epitaph to War* – hymn for choir page 86
- *The Blue Danube Waltz* by Johann Strauss page 91

PLOT OUTLINE

Bridie is in a television studio explaining Japanese torture

Bridie and Sheila are in the motel room

Sheila is nervous about the interview with Rick

They are evacuated from Singapore and the ships sunk

They argue about Sheila 'disappearing'

Become Japanese POW's

Lipstick Larry and the pin incident

The shoe-horn becomes the choir metronome

The women become closer in the motel room

The caramel and digger story

The truth about Sheila comes out

Many die on the trip to Belalau

Sheila tells of her life after the camps

They decide to continue singing and sing the sonata

(Sheila revisits the camp)

Bridie's DJ's theft story

Rescued and telling the truth about their stories

PLOT SUMMARY

ACT ONE SCENE ONE

The scene opens in darkness with only the voice of Bridie heard. The spotlight falls upon her as she outlines how the Japanese torture prisoners by making them kowtow (bow at the waist) for hours. Note here how she uses Japanese words to lend authenticity to her story. This makes us even more aware of her personal experience.

Bridie, we realise from the 'On-Air' sign is being interviewed and a male voice questions her about her role in the war. She had left Chatswood to seek some adventure as a young girl. She had wanted to follow in her father's footsteps as he had gone to WWI. It is here that we first get a mention of the shoehorn, which is the recurring image or motif in the text.

Bridie explains how she went to Singapore and found it very different from Australia. Here they had no idea that the Japanese were so dangerous, but this soon changed. The 'Japs' took Malaya and bombed Singapore. Bridie tells of the evacuation of Singapore, the crowded ships and the panic that occurred.

Forty-four ships left Singapore to sail to safety but they headed into the South China Sea where the Japanese destroyers were waiting for them. The scene ends with her repeating the date, Friday the thirteenth of February.

QUESTIONS FOR ACT ONE SCENE ONE

- What is your first impression of Bridie?
- Describe one of her early experiences in Singapore.
- How does her youthful naivety show?
- Read the playwright's notes at the end of the scene. Why do you think he adds this and makes it so prescriptive?

ACT ONE SCENE TWO

Scene Two opens in a motel room with the two women, Bridie and Sheila. The playwright's notes suggest, "There is a slight but obvious tension between them". They begin to talk about general trivia and then about Sheila's approaching interview.

Sheila is nervous about the interview but Bridie reassures her that Rick, the interviewer, only wants to know about the camps. They begin to catch up on their personal histories and mention the others who have also come to tell their story.

The tension between the two spills over when Bridie accuses Sheila of "hiding" from her. Bridie now knows that Sheila has been in Fremantle, Western Australia not England for all the post war years. The tension dissipates when they perform a coffin lifting ritual they learnt in the camps while lifting a bag in the room.

The scene ends with "Ya-Ta", a sound like a war cry which leads to a blackout on the stage. This ritual from the camp reveals how little they have forgotten.

QUESTIONS FOR ACT ONE SCENE TWO

- Why is there tension between Bridie and Sheila?
- How can we tell from this scene that they were close friends at the camp?
- The two women have been separated for fifty years. Why do you think that Sheila has not made contact with her friend for all those years?
- What does the ritual confirm about the two women?

ACT ONE SCENE THREE

Scene Three begins with the two women back in the studio and it is Sheila's turn to be interviewed. Bridie begins to interrupt but after the slides of the evacuation are flashed on the screen Sheila begins to tell her story of the evacuation. The visuals are a memory prompt.

She was fifteen when evacuated from Singapore on board a boat called the *Giang Bee*. The Japanese attacked this ship, Sheila was lost at sea and survived by hanging to a piece of wood for buoyancy. Covered in oil and very cold, she clung on for her life.

Bridie tells how the Japanese bombed her ship, the *Vyner Brooke,* and the lifeboats were shot at by Japanese planes. The life jackets the boat had been given were faulty and many women broke their necks jumping from the ship. So the rest of the women and children went down ropes to the sea. They also floated around the sea.

This is how the two women met, floating around in the South China Sea. They kept each other alive by talking to each other and Bridie also hit Sheila with the shoe-horn. This kept her awake although she said it hurt. A wave eventually separated the pair but they were reunited and picked up by a Japanese vessel.

Note that Misto picks up the theme song *Jerusalem* which is a very patriotic, British hymn and uses it to close the scene. He combined this with photos of the Japanese invading Singapore. This technique becomes the norm for scene closure. It helps the audience reflect on significant points in the script as well as assisting the audience to follow the course of the war.

QUESTIONS FOR ACT ONE SCENE THREE

- Choose either Bridie or Sheila's story and retell it in your own words. Limit this response to ten lines.
- Why does Bridie interrupt Sheila? What does this show about their relationship, even after many years have passed?
- The playwright includes extensive notes through this scene to ensure the performance is directed in a particular way. Choose one of the notes and describe the way in which you think it would impact an audience. Comment also on the purpose it plays in the text.

ACT ONE SCENE FOUR

Back at the motel Bridie and Sheila are discussing the day's events. Things become terse and they snap at and correct each other. They argue over Britain's role in the war and Sheila defends the Empire over Bridie's more pragmatic approach.

Sheila is about to leave but they continue to talk about the camp and the things that happened there. This includes making loincloths for the Japanese. They are united again at the end of the scene as they remember how Bridie sewed a rusty pin into 'Lipstick Larry's' loincloth. It sticks into him as he bows to the Japanese flag. Even though he hits Bridie it is the best moment of the war for them both. Memories provide shared visual images which unite them.

QUESTIONS FOR ACT ONE SCENE FOUR

- Why does Bridie mention the lice?
- In five lines describe the argument over British actions in the war. Use your own words.
- What items of food and drink does Sheila mention in this scene? What do these items suggest about conditions in the camp? Explain your answer fully.
- Compose the story of 'Lipstick Larry's Pin' from his point of view. Try to show your understanding of the Japanese and how they saw the POWs.

ACT ONE SCENE FIVE

The interviews resume at the beginning of this scene and Bridie and Sheila are now being interviewed together, "sitting side by side". They tell the story of how their friends made it to Radji Beach on Banka Island but were viciously murdered by the Japanese.

Bridie and Sheila were picked out of the water and taken to Sumatra (part of Indonesia) and placed in a camp. Conditions were extremely harsh and they used leaves for toilet paper. The food was 'rotten' and the women were so adversely affected, they stopped menstruating. They were beaten and some women chose to be used sexually by the Japanese, just so they could survive.

The Japanese created an 'officers club' and twelve nurses were told to attend. The Japanese tried to use them for sexual favours but they pretended to have tuberculosis and survived with their integrity intact.

They tell of how life was a real struggle in the camps. They shared everything, even a chop bone that they often gnawed. Many women died and some just went crazy and were shot. To improve morale the missionaries started a voice orchestra, as they had no instruments. They had a score where a woman's voice could be an instrument.

Bridie became a part of the voice orchestra as her shoe-horn became the metronome for the group. After eight weeks practising they sang Ravel's *Bolero*. They became free through the music, "Fifty voices and a shoe-horn."

QUESTIONS FOR ACT ONE SCENE FIVE

- What happened at Radji Beach?
- Describe the conditions at the camp. Use quotes from the text to support your response.
- What was Lavender Street?
- How do the girls escape having sexual relations with the Japanese?
- How did the choir begin and what did it achieve?

ACT ONE SCENE SIX

Scene Six begins in Sheila's motel suite. They two women are dancing and singing in a conga line. They are preparing to do this with the other girls from the camp, for Rick's show but Sheila is unsure. She is beginning to think she has told Rick a bit too much about the past.

They begin to argue about some of the other responses, especially over the sexual favours that some women gave the Japanese. Women used these favours to get food and survive. Bridie then sees some photos of a young Sheila and says she would like one for the memories of it all.

Bridie shows Sheila an old tobacco tin. It had contained food that Sheila had given her on her birthday when she was sick from dengue fever in the camp. Bridie shows that she truly cared for Sheila and is embarrassed.

They regather themselves and Bridie leaves. Sheila is now alone and goes to a drawer and gets a shoe-horn.

We then hear a voice over where a very young Sheila is made to sing for the Japanese.

The scene ends this way as we watch Sheila stare at the shoe-horn and two photos of the suffering women are shown on the screen.

QUESTIONS FOR ACT ONE SCENE SIX

- What impression of the two women do we get at the beginning of the scene?
- What is humorous about the song? What does it say about the women in the camp?
- Retell the birthday present story from Sheila's point of view.

- Why does Misto give us an impression of a young Sheila at the end of the scene? Does this change your opinion of Sheila? What impact do you think this would have on an audience?

ACT ONE SCENE SEVEN

The scene opens with photos of starving prisoners of war and the male voice-over asks, "Were you ever that bad?"

Bridie says in response that she got to five stone and Sheila four. They made wills just in case they died. Then she tells the story of the caramel and how they shared it a bit at a time. She concedes they eventually ate it in 1943. She goes on to tell that story.

At Christmas that year some Australian diggers who had left a work party serenaded them. The men sang them Christmas carols and one winked, and later waved, at Bridie.

The girls sang back to them and it was a relief from the drudgery and misery of the camp. The Japanese finally rounded up the men but it left a good feeling in the camp. This is when they ate the caramel, taking it in turns to suck it.

Bridie felt exceptionally good about the man waving at her and she married him after they met up at the end of the war.

QUESTIONS FOR ACT ONE SCENE SEVEN

- Misto keeps reminding the audience of how the women suffered. How does he do this at the beginning of Scene Seven and what effect do these constant reminders have?

- In fifty words describe what happened at Christmas in 1943.
- How did this incident affect Bridie?

ACT ONE SCENE EIGHT

The scene begins in Sheila's motel room again. Sheila has a hangover from a party the night before. The girls from the camp who were in the show got together and celebrated. Bridie helps Sheila and Sheila mentions that she has a drinking problem. They become uneasy with each other and begin to talk about the camp.

Bridie asks why Sheila didn't want to see her again. Sheila evades the question and Bridie tells her she was hurt. This is especially so after the previous night when Bridie said, "Don't come near me, Bridie." They begin to fight and Bridie slaps Sheila.

Sheila retaliates by going to the drawer and getting the shoe-horn and throwing it at Bridie. It is the shoe-horn from the camp that Bridie thought Sheila had swapped for the quinine that saved her life at Belalau camp. Sheila had looked after Bridie when she had a bad fever.

Sheila's story comes out. She had gone to Lipstick Larry and he gave her quinine for sexual favours after she had sung to the Japanese at Lavender Street. Bridie is stunned at this information and cannot respond.

The scene concludes with a young Sheila's voice coming in over the scene and Bridie turns to face Sheila with a response as the lights fade with a song.

QUESTIONS FOR ACT ONE SCENE EIGHT

- List what out of character activities Sheila did at the party the previous night. Does this affect our opinion of her?
- Does Sheila have a drinking problem? How do we know this?
- What reason does Sheila give for not contacting Bridie after the war?
- In your own words retell Sheila's story from the point where she goes to Lipstick Larry. You should try to convey some sense of her emotional state.
- Conflict is central to drama. Outline the conflict in *The Shoe-Horn Sonata* and say how it adds to the drama of the play as a whole.

END OF ACT ONE

ACT TWO SCENE NINE

Back at the television studio the scene opens to a back-drop of a huge photograph of a captured woman bowing to the Japanese. Bridie is singing the hymn the POW's sang at the time. The questioning gets back to Belalau.

Belalau was a rubber plantation cut off from the rest of the world. They had a terrible trip on a cattle boat to reach it and all the prisoners were in a shocking condition. Many died on the trip but there were individual acts of courage and bravery. One example was the nurse who washed the bedpans on the moving boat.

Many prisoners were being moved at this time because the Japanese had orders to kill all prisoners by October 1945. The Japanese now had a no work, no food policy and so many were left to starve to death. Their main job was grave digging and they did this on all fours, as they were too weak to stand. Sheila tells the story of how Bridie got sick and she saved her but she tells the version where she swaps the shoe-horn for the quinine tablets.

Sheila goes on to talk about how the Japanese lied about the course of the war and they rarely knew what was happening. The Japanese even claimed at one point that they had sunk the Sydney Harbour Bridge.

She also talks about the message that Prime Minister Curtin sent to them in the camp. He ordered the women to "keep smiling" and they all burst out laughing. The Japanese punished them severely for laughing but it continued.

The scene ends with a photo of Curtin looking distressed and two pictures of male POWs. The music is *When You're Smiling*.

QUESTIONS FOR ACT TWO SCENE NINE

- Describe Belalau.
- Retell the nurse and the 'bedpans' story from that nurse's point of view. Write about one hundred to one hundred and fifty words.
- Why do you think that the Japanese wanted to kill all the prisoners of war by October 1945?
- Why does Sheila not tell the whole truth in her story?
- What is ironic about the message from Prime Minister Curtin?
- What symbolism is depicted in the background images?

ACT TWO SCENE TEN

The same photo of starving, male POWs is still in view. Sheila is doing some needlework. Bridie tells her she is missing lunch but Sheila says she can't stand rice. They talk about how thin they were and how the interviews are nearly over.

Bridie asks Sheila if she will be all right and they talk about their lives. There is still tension in the relationship but it now revolves around what Sheila did for Bridie when she saved her life. Sheila says she tried to tell her the truth before, in Singapore after they were rescued, but couldn't as Bridie was sick.

They talk at length about the incident and how it has affected Sheila's life. She left Singapore for Australia and got used to the country in time. Sheila then tells Bridie that she had to go with the 'Jap' as she couldn't just let her die. She also confesses she nearly told her mother the truth but her mother had said, "We must pull up our socks and get on with it."

Bridie had tried to protect Sheila but sees it all now as a failure. Bridie is distressed and says, "You should have let me die." The tension is broken by a bright male voice asking, "Hello ladies! Did you have a nice lunch?"

The two women realise their microphones have been on and wonder if they have been overheard. The song *I'll Walk Alone* plays.

QUESTIONS FOR ACT TWO SCENE TEN

- Why do you think Sheila doesn't like rice?
- What has happened in Sheila's life in the years after the war?
- Why didn't Sheila tell Bridie about how she saved her in Singapore?
- How does Misto increase the tension and conflict in this scene?
- What breaks the tension between the two women and unites them again?

ACT TWO SCENE ELEVEN

Still in the studio the two women are talking about the postcards they received after a wait of two years. They can still remember what was written on them. The stage darkens and the dialogue resumes with the story of the death of Mrs Dryburgh and the end of the choir.

The two women then decided to continue performing music and think of a sonata – a piece for two instruments. They, of course, use their two voices. They had four songs which they sang while they dug graves. Bridie would tap out a rhythm – "waving the shoe-horn." They sang it to the camp and it was something the Japanese couldn't take away.

Sheila tells of how she went back to the camp once whilst on holidays. The camp was gone and she couldn't find the graves of her friends who were buried on its outskirts. She recalls how the nurse's bodies were taken home but they left the civilian women and children behind. She says she went back because she had "never really left".

The stage darkens again and Bridie tells of how they were given thirty pounds compensation. This was for the time that they spent in the camp. The wanted more but the Australian Government wouldn't help them at all.

QUESTIONS FOR ACT TWO SCENE ELEVEN

- Why do you think the Japanese took two years to deliver the mail?
- Imagine you are the parent of a POW in Belalau. Compose twenty words that you would write on a postcard to your daughter.
- What is a sonata?
- List the four songs that they practised.
- Why do you think that Sheila went back to the camp? What effect did this journey have on her?
- The camp no longer exists but the play depicts life there. How does the play convey a distinctively visual experience of life in a long gone place and time?

ACT TWO SCENE TWELVE

Bridie and Sheila are entering the motel room and arguing again at the beginning of the scene. They are arguing about the future and about the past. They find some common ground in talking about the guards at the camp. Bridie tells how she was terrified of them although she put on a brave face.

Bridie then relates an incident where she was shopping at David Jones Food Hall. She had some shortbread when some Japanese tourists came in and surrounded her. She got frightened and ran out with the biscuits and was arrested for shop lifting. She was too scared to tell the truth so she was fined in court. She is still "cringing with shame" at the thought of it.

Sheila replies that keeping a secret is wearing on the body and soul, so why keep one? Bridie says it is best so that other people don't know but Sheila has come to the conclusion that the survivors are more important.

They begin to argue about the truth and how much difference one person can make. Sheila wants to tell the truth but Bridie say they will call her "a whore". Bridie takes her biscuits and leaves. Sheila mimics a chook and darkness falls.

Again Misto uses the screen and song to add to the scene at its conclusion. Here we have the faces of WWII political leaders and a song "about secret and forbidden love".

QUESTIONS FOR ACT TWO SCENE TWELVE

- List the things that Bridie and Sheila argue about in this scene.

- Why is Bridie's theft story amusing? What does it add to her characterisation?
- Why does Sheila want to tell the truth? Do you think she should tell the truth? Why/Why not? As an activity compose a letter to Sheila outlining your argument.

ACT TWO SCENE THIRTEEN

The studio 'On-Air' light is on and Bridie and Sheila begin to talk about the end of the war. They tell how many women kept diaries although it was very dangerous and even led to death at the hands of the Japanese. They kept them because they wanted their families to know about what had happened to them. At the end of the war the British took their diaries and burnt them, not wanting the world to know what had happened to them.

The Japanese continued to be cruel right to the very end of the war, hoping that most prisoners would die. One morning they got all the women out of bed and took them out. Most thought they were going to be shot. Instead, they had been gathered to listen to a Japanese Army brass band. It was their little bit of culture for the war as defined by the Geneva Convention. It was at this point that they began to think they might live.

At the end of the war the camp was only found because an Australian journalist had heard about a secret camp. He persisted and found them on the 24th of August 1945. They had been prisoners for "one thousand two hundred and eighty seven days", when the Japanese abandoned the camp. The gate to the camp was open and they had to get up the courage to walk into the local village. They made it, together, by helping each other.

Both women then retell the stories they had told earlier, but this time they tell the truth. Bridie tells the truth about Sheila and the Japanese guard and Sheila tells why Bridie was arrested. The truth comes out and the scene fades to darkness.

Misto again uses the screen and music to reinforce his point with recovering nurses on the screen and the song *Epitaph to War*.

QUESTIONS FOR ACT TWO SCENE FOURTEEN

- Why are the Japanese destroying diaries and punishing those who keep them?
- Why do you think the British lie to the women?
- Why do the Japanese allow the band to play?
- Who finds the nurses and how?
- Imagine you are either Bridie or Sheila. Describe how you get to the village and how you felt.
- Why do they tell the truth at the end of the scene? What effect does this have on our perception of them? What does it say about their relationship?

ACT TWO SCENE FOURTEEN

Again we are in Sheila's motel room and Bridie comes in. They both come together when they have to lift the suitcase, reflecting an earlier scene. When Sheila finds the motel is owned by the Japanese she begins to take things to get them back.

Bridie gives Sheila her address and tells her to keep in touch. Sheila, to Bridie's surprise, said she might visit for Christmas. Sheila offers the shoe-horn to Bridie. She hesitates but accepts.

They dance as Bridie had promised at the end of the war. The last dialogue is Bridie saying, "Sheila Richards – you're a whinging bloody Pom."

Again music (*The Blue Danube*) plays and as they dance "the stage gradually grows darker and darker" only the shoe-horn is in light.

QUESTIONS FOR ACT TWO SCENE FOURTEEN

- How does the suitcase incident unite them?
- Why is Bridie surprised that Sheila suggests a visit?
- Why do they dance?
- The shoe-horn is the last thing that the audience sees. Why do you think Misto structures the scene this way?

END OF PLAY

Women kow towing to Japanese
BBC News Oct 19th 2014.

SETTING

- Japan
- Malaya
- Singapore
- Sumatra
- P.O.W. Camps

Japan

The local name for this country that comprises four large islands (Hokkaido, Honshu, Kyushu, Shikoku) and other smaller islands is Nippon. The country is situated in the Pacific Ocean and its nearest neighbours are Korea, China and Russia.

Japan, a country of limited natural resources, now relies on major industry such as electronics, vehicles and shipbuilding for jobs and income. It has a long history but little contact was made with the west until the Meiji Restoration in 1868.

After this time, Japan began to have military ambitions. Wars with China 1894–5, Russia 1904–5, Korea 1910 and China 1931–2 and 1937 occurred. During these wars Japan conquered much land and developed a warlike reputation under their Emperor who was the Head of State.

In 1941 the Japanese attacked Pearl Harbour in Hawaii and they began to push through the countries in South East Asia including Burma, Malaya, Singapore, and the countries now called Indonesia and Papua New Guinea. Darwin was bombed and midget submarines were found in Sydney Harbour. japan was finally defeated when the Americans dropped the atomic bomb on Hiroshima and Nagasaki in 1945.

Malaya

Now better known as Malaysia, Malaya's closest sea was the South China Sea, off the Malay Peninsula. To its north lies Thailand and at its tip, Singapore. Kuala Lumpur is the capital of Malaysia. The main language is Malay but Chinese, English and Tamil are widely spoken. Its tropical climate lent itself to the success of large rubber plantations under British rule. Today those plantations and much of the jungle have been used for growing palm oil.

The strong British influence in the country since the early 1600s survived but was weakened by the Japanese invasion and occupation in World War Two. At the war's end the Malay States were federated and the country was independent by 1957. Malaysia was formed in 1963 with British North Borneo: Sabah, Sarawak and Singapore joining the federated states. In 1965 Singapore left the federation and became a country in its own right.

The country's economy now relies on natural and energy resources, electronic components, electrical goods and tourism. It is now a constitutional monarchy.

Singapore

Singapore (Republic of Singapore) is an island on the southern tip of Malaysia. It became an independent state in 1965 after briefly federating with Malaysia. The capital is Singapore City. It is a tiny state only 618 square kilometres in size.

Sir Stamford Raffles is one of the famous British names associated with the country. He arrived in Singapore in January 1819, saw potential for the island and helped negotiate a treaty with the local rulers to establish Singapore as a trading station. The city quickly grew as a trading hub, attracting immigrants from China, India, the Malay Archipelago and beyond. It remained a British colony until 1942.

In 1942 the Japanese invaded through Malaya and occupied the country until 1945. During occupation the Japanese held many British and Australian prisoners of war (POWs) captured during the invasion. Singapore (and Malaysia) still maintain and remember much of the history of the Japanese invasion. Museums housing photographs and other visual artefacts help preserve and pass on memories.

Sumatra

Sumatra, to the south of Singapore, is now part of Indonesia. It is only a short distance from Singapore across the Strait of Malacca. There has been a strong separatist movement on the island since 1949 when the Indonesians gained independence and control.

The island is about one third swamp and marshland and it has abundant natural resources. Agriculture is one of the chief occupations.

P.O.W. Camps

The Japanese had a poor attitude to prisoners from the beginning of the war. Part of this was cultural as they saw that all people who had surrendered were cowards and thus deserved any treatment that was given to them. It is also known that while the Japanese signed the Geneva Convention on the care of prisoners they did not ratify it and felt no binding rules applied to them, especially when they were winning.

Cruelty and brutality were encouraged and beatings were common for both women and men. Both sexes, while separated, were made to work for food and this food was of poor quality.

Food was generally a portion of rice that was steamed and occasionally some broth or fish heads. Prisoners ate scraps left by the guards and any wildlife including insects and frogs. Disease became common and all suffered from malnutrition and complaints such as beriberi.

Latrines (toilets) were substandard and were maintained by the prisoners most of whom had diarrhoea and other digestive tract problems. Poor food and hard work contributed to illness. When disease became a problem Japanese held back the drugs given by the Red Cross so the prisoners would die or they used them for currency. No parcels or mail were issued in many camps until the end of the war.

The accommodation was often in the form of huts, which were leaky, poorly maintained and open to the elements. Complaints were met with violence and beatings with bamboo canes. Prisoners were also put in isolation cages and left to die.

Transportation between camps was always crowded and uncomfortable. Occasionally trucks were used but walking was common. The dead were just left by the roadside. Movement by ship was also used and Misto describes this in the play. Often no food or water was given on trips and many died, especially from the heat, combined with disease.

There can be no doubt the description of events that Misto portrays in *The Shoe-Horn Sonata* are realistic and create strong visual images. Evidence supports the types of incidents told by the women in their interviews. The Japanese were exceptionally cruel to prisoners of war and callous and indifferent attitudes were partly cultural but were also seen as malicious.

There are many incidents recorded of exceptionally cruel and barbaric individuals who enjoyed inflicting pain. Additionally, it was quite common for women to be raped and murdered by the invaders. This setting must have been one of horror and it is great credit to anyone who survived for so long in these conditions.

Misto has certainly captured the reality of the war time setting through not only the stories but also the descriptions. He emphasises the conditions through the use of slides and photos. In exploring the Distinctively Visual in relation to this play, the stories and descriptive language as well as the visual images portrayed through slides and photos, serve to create a picture of the conditions for POWs. Analyse these in detail and ensure you can talk about them, in detail, referencing techniques in your responses.

QUESTIONS FOR SETTING

- Find a map of South East Asia and identify the key settings in the story.
- Use the internet to find some photos of prisoners of war who were held in the Pacific by the Japanese. While you may well be familiar with the Jewish concentration camp photos, these are equally disturbing. They will give you a visual picture of what Bridie and Sheila suffered.

- Find a picture of some camp accommodation. In fifty words describe this accommodation. Try to focus on what you can see, not what you know from the text.

CHARACTER ANALYSIS

- **Bridie**
- **Sheila**
- **Rick's voice**
- **Other characters**

Bridie

Bridie is an Australian woman who grew up in Chatswood on the North Shore of Sydney, New South Wales. At the time the play is set she would be in her seventies. She is the first character we see in *The Shoe-Horn Sonata* and she establishes the format for the studio scenes in the play.

Bridie, unlike Sheila, chose to be in Singapore for the war. She questions this choice later when in the camps,

> *"I'd stare at the dirt and ask myself why I'd ever left Chatswood in the first place."*

Bridie chose to go to the war because her father had fought in Egypt and it seemed like an adventure. She recalls that he was proud of her for going. Her posting to Johore Bahru in Singapore was an exciting adventure because,

> *"I'd never been further than Woy Woy."*

Things changed rapidly for her. She appears perceptive about British inadequacies and foibles during the Japanese invasion. This is clear by her recount of the British considering shooting all the nurses to save them from rape by the Japanese (p.21).

Bridie has excellent recall and we see that in the detail she recounts even though it is an emotional tale and a long time has passed. Over time, she developed her own strategies for coping. Her recounting of the stories from the camps is seemingly accurate and only Sheila questions some perspectives, not incidents. that Bridie's particular perspective reflects how she sees things. It is perfectly normal in a series of personal anecdotes.

It is interesting to note through her narrative that she does not hate the Japanese

"I'll forgive the Japs for what they did to us in camp"

However, she leaves nothing to the imagination in describing the horrors that she suffered. This is balanced to some extent by the joy of some incidents such as the caramel, the pin in the pants of Larry and the carols involving male prisoners from another camp.

It is during carols she saw her future husband in the ranks of the male prisoners of war. He waved and winked at her and she confesses,

"After the war I married him"

Bridies' release from captivity in the camp was just the beginning of her rehabilitation. The tale of her walk to the village from the camp is a story of survival on its own, revealing true courage and a survival instinct. The parallel sentences and repetition of "dragged" provides a visual image of the two women's co-dependency as they struggled from confinement.

"Sometimes I dragged Sheila. Sometimes Sheila dragged me. The main thing is we got there. And we could never have done that alone."

This quote not only touches on Bridie's courage but also illuminates points about the relationship of the two women at the time and how they relied on each other for survival and support. This is a time when they had been together for so long.

Even after they returned to Singapore Bridie was suffering from the effects of the conditions in the camps. Her chest had been x-rayed and she had been diagnosed with TB (tuberculosis) and it was thought that she had only five years to live. But Bridie proves her toughness and survival skills by saying "dismissively,"

"It takes more than TB to get me!"

This is Bridie's view of herself, a tough and strong survivor, who helped Sheila make it through the war because of how she took control with her pragmatic approach. This perception of herself is altered dramatically when Sheila informs her how she saved her life in Belalau. Bridie's view of herself and the view conveyed to the audience helps paint a distinctively visual portrait of this imagined character.

Bridie was dying when Sheila used her body to procure drugs from the Japanese to save Bridie's life. This alters both Bridie's perception of herself but also how she relates to Sheila. Bridie seems to be the dominant character and we know this from the way she acts and how she interrupts Sheila and bullies her to some extent. However, time and knowledge have changed this and Bridie's views are able to change too.

For example she is very much against women selling themselves for food,

"I didn't. To go with a Jap—to give him pleasure—how could you ever live with yourself."

She is unforgiving in this regard and maintains this view throughout the war and until she meets Sheila again. It is only when she learns that Sheila has sold herself that she reconsiders, after her initial horror. She thinks that if Sheila tells the truth,

"You know what they'll call you. They'll call you a whore."

By the conclusion of the play she has come to terms with what Sheila has done and to some extent made peace with herself.

"she sold herself to him for tablets. She was a beautiful, kind and brave young woman. She wasn't just my friend—she was—she is— the other half of my life."

Bridie has finally come to terms with what survival is and what truth means. She hasn't completely changed but has evolved into a more understanding individual who allows shades rather than just seeing the world in absolute terms. The unfolding of the truth has helped shape a clear picture of the woman and the situation.

Bridie's anger at Sheila for not contacting her for all the years after the war has dissipated in this understanding. She is happy to have Sheila visit and has accepted the shoe-horn in the final scene as a sign of reconciliation. The final dance confirms things have come full circle for them. But Bridie never loses her core identity, the one that kept her going through the war. We see this in the final comment that is said tenderly,

>*"Sheila Richards—you're a whinging bloody Pom!"*

Character Quote

>*"We fought all the time. You were worse than my mother"*

CHARACTER QUESTIONS FOR BRIDIE

- Create a list of ten words or phrases that you could use to describe Bridie's personality.

Select three of these words and find an example and/or quote from the text to support your word or phrase.

- What tells us in the first scene of the play that Bridie is an Australian? In your response list some of the language clues.
- Why does Bridie go to war?
- What is her reaction to Singapore?
- How does she view the British?
- What qualities does she show by surviving in the water?
- How important do you think her sense of humour is in surviving? Find an example of her idea of humour.
- How does she save Sheila in the water?
- Why do you think Bridie and Sheila become an inseparable team in the camps? What role does Bridie take up?

- Do you think time has changed Bridie at all? If so in what way since the war.
- How has her relationship with Sheila changed? You might like to think about the power in the relationship.
- In what way does Sheila's revelation change things?
- In a letter to Sheila in Fremantle, three months after the show has gone to air, write how you, Bridie, feel about things now. Comment on how you feel about Sheila and your own life now.

Sheila

Sheila is younger than Bridie as she was only fifteen when the Japanese invaded Singapore and she was taken captive. Although she has lived in Fremantle, Australia since the end of the war she is still very British. This British part of her has never been lost and shows through during the play in her attitudes to situations and events.

An example of this is when early in the play she rebuts Bridie's remark that the British were "thick". She responds

> *"We were patriotic. We didn't want to leave. I remember mother saying, 'Sheila, you and I are English women. We do not run away from a few Orientals.'"*

Her mother also gives her some useless advice more suited to the old world and another time and place in,

> *"set a good example, Always wear gloves – wherever you go. Don't socialise with Catholics…And never kiss an Australian on the lips."*

Sheila and Bridie continue to disagree on things British through the play because Bridie does not have the illusions that Sheila was raised with. We can see the effect of Sheila's sheltered life on both her attitudes during the early part of her captivity and even after the war has ended. Her mother, who she tries to tell about Lipstick Larry, just wants to carry on in true British spirit despite what has happened

"You know what the Bible says my dear. 'No cross, no crown.' We must pull up our socks and get on with it."

In her adult life Sheila has tried to continue with this attitude but it has marked her adult life adversely. She seems unhappy and bitter as we see when she gets drunk. Sheila has repressed much of her that is good in order to survive. She has an ordered life with a job as a librarian and she has never married. The secret she has kept since the war has eaten away at her and it has not brought her any happiness.

The chance to tell her story at first frightens her because she is afraid of what the consequences might be. She even threatens to turn her hearing aid off if the questions become too complex and personal. She begins the interviews nervously,

"Hello? Can you hear me?"

but this soon changes as she begins to tell her stories of life in the camps. Again, later, she begins to think that she has said too much at one point before deciding to tell the complete truth, difficult though it may be. This is especially so about the story of how she saved Bridie's life, even though Bridie tells it to the cameras. Bridie helps her by saying,

"That isn't the truth, love... Do you want me to tell the truth?"

Sheila confirms this with a nod and it seems like a huge relief for her. This incident has been a huge psychological block for her over time.

The war has left both physical and psychological scars and these are shown in smaller incidents. For example she has never been able to form relationships.

> *"You mean 'Did I ever have lovers?' I didn't really mind. Mother always used to say that sex was like a trip to Brighton. Took you ages to get there and it wasn't worth the trouble. Even she drew the line at doing it for England."*

Sheila also journeys back to the camp to see if she can come to some form of understanding about what happened and her life.

> *"Once in my holidays – I went back to the camp. I'd spent thirty years running away from it – not telling a soul – trying to forget."*

Sheila feels she has

> *"never really left."*

Telling her story in a sympathetic environment helps her to accept what has happened.

Sheila, however, is not the same girl as she was when she first met Bridie and the relationship now seems on a more even level. They disagree as they always did but now Bridie does not seem the leader as she was then. At the play's end harmony is reached as they come to some understanding about where they are now rather than where they were.

The initial scenes where they fight and disagree creates tension and conflict in the play. This conflict and tension are released as both women realise that it is the secrets that they carry, not each other, that are the problem. Sheila releases her tension negatively at one point when she drinks heavily at the reunion party. She dances on the table and sings 'God Save the Queen'. She also does some silly re-enactments from the camp. She admits she may have gone too far.

But this is only temporary and she works through her problems during the interviews and conversations back at the motel. She comes to realise that she can be friends with Bridie. Her life in Fremantle can still go on but it has been expanded rather than narrowed by her most recent experiences.

Giving the shoe-horn to Bridie in the final scene of Act One (scene 8) is a catalyst for release of Sheila's tension and it is symbolic of her holding on to the past. Indeed, she doesn't really give it to Bridie but

> "Sheila takes the shoe-horn out of the drawer and throws it onto the bed"

Contrast this with the final scene of Act Two when Sheila holds the shoe-horn out to Bridie and says

> "Go on". [Take it]

The final scene is a far more controlled one and it shows a more empathic Sheila and a more accepting Bridie. It reveals how far they have come.

Sheila and Bridie were united during the war and have now come together again. Sheila takes the promise of a dance that Bridie offered her in Belalau and claims it now as the shoe-horn is put to the side.

Character Quote

> *"One never stops being British. Nor does one want to".*

CHARACTER QUESTIONS FOR SHEILA

- What is Sheila's initial reaction to being interviewed?
- Give a short summary of Sheila's upbringing.
- What effect do you think her British upbringing has had on her life? Use some specific examples or quotes to support your response.
- Why is there conflict between Bridie and Sheila early in the play?
- Why do you think Sheila has 'hidden' from Bridie for all the post war years?
- What was her reason for doing what she did to save Bridie? What do you think of her decision? Do you think you could have made that decision?
- Do you think her trip back to the camp was a good idea? What effect did it have on her? What is Misto trying to tell his audience in this section of the play?
- How has their relationship changed over time? Do you think they end the play on equal terms?
- Describe what you think the future holds for Sheila.

Rick's voice

Rick's voice is the only male voice in the play and is not a character in the true sense. Rick is talked about by the two main characters. Bridie says,

> "He just wants to hear stories from the camp. ... Don't worry. He's very tactful."

> "Rick's delighted with the show. He's strutting round downstairs like the cat that licked the -[cream]"

What we do get from Rick are lots of questions. It must be remembered that the purpose he has for the women is to get their story and even if he is sympathetic it is a job for him. He is the force that brings them together and controls their stories. It is, in turn, through these collective stories that the Distinctively Visual is created and responders picture a perspective of war.

It seems as if Misto is still giving the male power over the women and the control, much like in the camps and in life. While they get to tell their story it is for a purpose and he uses his power to manipulate. He is never seen, only heard, and this unseen manipulation is how the women have always suffered.

While Rick is the catalyst that brings the women together again, he may not be the benign force that the women see him as at times. It is probable Rick certainly shows more understanding in his questions as the interviews proceed but this may just be more that the stories are so shocking and sad that he responds to this to create better television.

Character Quote

"He's not like Donohue, is he? Strutting around like a turkey on heat"

CHARACTER QUESTIONS FOR RICK

- Why do you think a male interviewer, Rick, is used by Misto rather than a female?
- What impression do you get from Rick through his questions?

Other characters

Other characters mentioned in the play also have roles to fill although they are not seen or heard. There are more characters that shed some light on our two main characters.

These characters would be

- Bridie's father
- Sheila's mother
- Lipstick Larry

Also the women from the camps mentioned in the play make the audience visualise the shared experience.

These are

- Myra
- Joyce
- Irene
- Ivy (dead)
- Ava

QUESTION FOR OTHER CHARACTERS

- Choose one character from the first list and say how they contribute to our understanding of either Sheila or Bridie.

THEMES

- Distinctively Visual
- History and Memory
- Truth
- Power
- Relationships
- War

Distinctively Visual

While not specifically a thematic concern or idea Distinctively Visual has been placed in this section, as it is the main focus of your studies in this module. The module outline suggests that 'students explore the ways the images we see and/or visualise in texts are created.' Rather than identify, students must explore how these images affect how we see ideas in the text and how, in turn, these help shape meaning.

Think about the issue of visual images in the text and form some opinions of your own. To help you should have a clear understanding of dramatic techniques and especially read that section which follows the themes in this study guide. This will highlight specific things to look for and specific examples when discussing the formation of visual imagery.

Try to examine how Misto achieves these distinctively visual elements and how and where they are placed in the play. Apart from the spoken narratives, these can generally be described as the images that are shown in the background throughout the play. They should not be discussed in isolation, however, and should be considered in relation to the play as a whole. In many ways, in the theatre, you are watching a play within a play when the characters are in the studio. For example a playwright instruction such as,

> "the Japanese flag fades and we see photographs of the Japanese invasion of Singapore – Japanese soldiers riding bicycles, a sky filled with parachutes; Japanese battalions marching through the streets. As the song reaches its climax, we see hundreds of victorious Japanese soldiers, their arms raised in triumph, performing a Bonzai! Salute.
>
> It is a most disturbing sight. For this photograph has captured the moment when the British Empire teetered and fell..." (p.36)

In isolation this is not as effective as when it is combined with the ideas that have come before and after. In other words you need to have the contextual framework to make it work as it does in the play. This is a crucial moment in the play and also in the history of Australia and it finishes a scene. This gives an added dramatic impact for an audience who have seen some positive images prior to this but have been guided to this point by the "blood red rising sun" of the Japanese flag that has been illuminated in the background. This is a clever dramatic technique and emphasises the complete change that these women must have undergone. No one had any understanding of what was about to occur. They lived through the fall of an Empire that had seemed indestructible. From here Misto focuses more on the personal triumphs and tragedies of the two characters and their relationship. Discussion of the following themes also incorporates the visual elements that help shape meaning and provide clarity for viewers.

As you study *The Shoe-Horn Sonata,* find your own example, place it in context and show what it achieves in terms of audience response. Look for examples where silence is used as this can often be more effective than dialogue or music as it emphasises the visual. Music can also be used in juxtaposition with the images to give the audience immediate contrast or to enhance the effectiveness of the images,

> *"Darkness. Two photographs of war-time Prime Minister John Curtin appear on screen. He looks quite distressed. These are followed by two photographs of emaciated male prisoners of war, starving, dying and covered in tropical ulcers. On the soundtrack we hear Judy Garland singing, 'When You're Smiling'..." (p.69)*

Here the juxtaposition of images creates powerful messages and irony is used to highlight the horror and isolation of victims of war.

Remember when you look for your related texts they do not have to be about the war or nurses or anything linked to the play. Choose some other textual form so you can show a range of knowledge and techniques. What the connection must be is the distinctively visual features the texts have. This means they don't have to be connected by content but can be connected by technique, effect, visual feature or any idea that you could reasonably link in. Having said that, while the visual imagery and images combine in this play to convey a war situation, texts such as Nick Ut's iconic 'Napalm Girl' or a film like *The Railway Man* (2013) also serve to capture the horror and brutality of war. Other suggested related texts are listed at the back of this volume.

QUESTIONS FOR DISTINCTIVELY VISUAL

- Choose one visual technique that Misto uses. Place it in context and show what effect it might have on an audience.

- Link another visual technique that Misto uses to enhance the theatricality of the play. Imagine you are in the audience watching. Think about the effect it might have on you and discuss how this may differ from the impact that the playwright desired.
- Discuss the use of music and image in the play. How does what we hear compare/ contrast to what we see?

History and Memory

History is, in some sense, what the play is about. It is, of course, about the histories of the women, the nurses that were captured by the Japanese during World War Two. It is about their individual histories and their joint suffering. While these stories are difficult to comprehend and are small histories in themselves, another factor that must be considered is the larger historical picture. Through story and imagery; visuals and images, a distinctive picture is drawn for the audience, of the horror of being a female POW in a Japanese camp during WWII.

This vignette picture of history is revealed as the story/ picture of the women slowly unfolds. It has not been made official and there is no government recognition of their plight and few, if any, official records. These painful memories are not part of any 'official' history and this is made clear in the play.

"The British didn't want anyone to know about us. They'd have lost prestige if people found out how women of the Empire had lived in the war. So for the sake of the King and Country, they burned our diaries. Every last one."

Prior to this the Japanese had tried to destroy all the diaries so that no record of how they had treated the women and children were recorded. They needed the history destroyed because of the fear of war crimes trials at the end of the war. This is also why they tried to kill all the women and children near the end of the war.

Misto makes it clear in the course of the play that the memories of the women are accurate although they may have some bias as all anecdotal evidence does. The oral stories from these fictional characters have juxtaposed and overlaid, the factual images to confirm and extrapolate the stories of the women. The visual images of the thin, starving people are very strong and clear to an audience. This is part of Misto's theatricality. It is worth taking some specific images and analysing them closely in terms of visual literacy techniques, such as salience, vectors, gaze and framing.

While it is considered that the writing of history belongs to the victors, in this case both the victors and the defeated tried to hide the truth, especially the horrific details that so shock us when revealed in the text. Even the silence of the women who seem afraid to tell their stories has helped keep the whole situation a secret since the war.

It is also not certain if Rick wants their memories for historical documentation or for gain. The media is particularly selective in what it uses and what makes good television is not necessarily what makes good, accurate history. Also the choices of Bridie and Sheila may be selective and we do not hear the stories of the other women. Rick controls what people will see and hear in the final cut of the show.

History and memory, as Misto shows, can be both selective and nonrepresentative. There are many reasons for this and Misto has set out to right what he sees as an error of omission by the government. Thus, he has made the hidden visual, both literally and metaphorically. In representing and telling the POW's stories, Misto uses Bridie and Sheila to point out the inadequacies of the government.

Sheila:

"We tried to fight for more but… the government has opposed us."

Bridie:

"No. The Australian Government. They told us we were on our own. Just like they told us once to keep smiling."

History and memory play an important role in the text and highlight how manipulation and deliberate omission are the realm of governments intent on hiding the truth. Thus, a clear and distinctively visual image emerges of incompetence and lack of compassion at a political level. Misto has given picture to what was hidden.

Theme Quote

"Not a headstone or memorial anywhere. Not even a cross survived the war."

The use of a negative anaphora in the above example, strengthens the message of a lack of care from a governmental level. Rather than visual imagery, the distinct omission of it highlights the fact that these POW's stories were not represented. The Distinctively visual is about seeing events, personalities and situations clearly and transparently. Is it Misto's aim to highlight a lack of transparency around his topic and to offer other ways of seeing?

THEME QUESTIONS

- Why did all three governments British, Australian and Japanese try to hide the truth about conditions in the camps?
- Why do you think they tried to manipulate history in this way?
- The women are reticent to tell their stories. Why do you think this is so? You might like to refer to Bridie and Sheila in particular in your response.
- Do you think there is a particular reason for the women's stories being kept secret while male POW stories are well documented?

Truth

There is a common quote, 'truth is the first casualty of war' and in the case of the stories revealed in *The* Shoe-Horn Sonata, it appears to be true. The central tenet of the play is that truth has not been told on many levels and this is another core aspect of the play.

The truth has not been told in many ways and the main offenders are,

- The British government
- The Australian government
- The Japanese government

And on a smaller but no less important level

- ◼ Sheila
- ◼ Bridie

The main reason for concealment of the truth is that it is too shocking for people to hear but this reasoning is shown to be false in the play. We expect the lies of governments and they often twist the truth to portray events as positively as possible. But the lesson of the play is that no matter how they try to conceal, the truth will come out. The truth will be seen clearly at the end. Consider this as an aspect of the Distinctively Visual.

Important to the play are the scenes where, on this more personal level, Bridie and Sheila reveal the truth. Sheila at first used her physical isolation on the other side of the country to keep her secret and stay away from Bridie but it hindered her life. Sheila's secret is so well hidden that Bridie, whose life she saved, has no idea of it. Bridie, on the other hand, keeps her secret because of the shame she feels and the effect that others knowing will bring to her.

Both women, when the truth is revealed, are able to open up to each other and have some reconciliation with themselves, each other and even the world around them. Both women take a while to get to this point in the course of the play but Misto keeps reminding us about truth through the play. For example:

"It was the biggest lie I've ever told. I was trying to keep you afloat."

"That isn't the truth. Love... Do you want me to tell the truth."

Truth is central to the issues in the play and should be considered in any analysis of the text.

Theme Quote

"And if the only way to get it is to tell the truth then—"

THEME QUESTIONS

- Misto shows that it is important for governments to tell the truth. How does he do this theatrically? You may wish to consider the use of the images on the screen and music as well as the dialogue.
- Why is it important that Bridie tells the truth? In your response allude to both her character and the audience's reaction to the truth.
- Why is it important that Sheila tells the truth? In your response allude to both her character and the audience's reaction to the truth.
- Distinctively Visual is about imagery and images which, rather than conceal, reveal the truth. Discuss.

Power

The Shoe-Horn Sonata deals with a number of power issues which revolve around specific areas. The first is the power between countries and how they use that power. We first see the British as the nation in power. They not only have their 'Empire' but are also a major colonial power in the region. They look down upon the Japanese.

When Singapore falls to the Japanese it seems that this is the end, psychologically, of the British Empire. It was unthinkable that they could lose the war. Bridie sums this up when she says;

"I remember I asked an Englishman once – a captain with a huge moustache – how dangerous the Japanese really were. 'My dear,' he said. 'They have slanty eyes. If they can't see properly how can they shoot?"

This level of arrogance and complete misconception led to the fall of all British colonies in the Far East and the Japanese Empire taking over in their own play for power. It is worth noting here that these 'Empires' seem male dominated and women play little role in any proceedings. This helps us understand why the women POW's were treated badly by both powers.

When the Japanese became the occupying force they are just as arrogant and unsympathetic and very much crueller. When they too are finally beaten at the end of the war they cannot seem to understand how it happened. Both the British and the Japanese abuse their power when in control and it reflects poorly on both nations.

On another level we can see the abuse of power between the prison guards and prisoners. The guards abused their power physically, sexually and emotionally and many seemed to enjoy the pain they inflicted. Lipstick Larry's comment

"Plenty of room in the graveyard for her"

attests to the physical and mental cruelty the guards exhibit. We can also see this in the Japanese Command that,

"Every prisoner of war – man, woman and child – was to die by October 1945. By bullet or sword or hunger or poison. They were taking us inland – where we'd never be found."

The prisoners had little option but to cooperate, be humiliated and abused. This abuse of power by the Japanese is documented in several incidents in the text. In such a way a distinctively visual image of the situation is accumulated.

On an individual level the relationship between Bridie and Sheila is worth examining in terms of power. During the war Bridie, as the older of the two, seems to be in charge and leads the way. She makes Sheila drink the charcoal water and acts as a surrogate mother at times.

By the end of the war they have become inseparable and Sheila has sold her body to save Bridie. Their walk to the village after their release shows their relationship to be more balanced with their reliance on each other.

Rick's documentary brings them together again many years after the war and Bridie again tries to take the dominant role. However, circumstance and time have changed things and they are now on level terms although Bridie still would like to be in charge.

It may be worth noting here that Rick, a male, still has the power over the women to some extent. He is in charge and has organised them all to be there. Bridie and Sheila even worry that he might have secretly overheard them when they are talking through lunch.

'Bridie and Sheila look up startled. Then they both realise they are wearing small microphones. They both wonder whether every word has been overheard.'

Here a male is still the dominant force in their lives and nothing seems to have changed in that regard since the war. They have little power or influence.

Power is an important element seen in the play and Misto gives us some new insights into its use and abuse in this context. The concept is conveyed distinctively and visually through techniques such as symbolism. The kow towing women portray this.

Theme Quote

> *"But I reminded myself that I was a woman of the Empire. And it wasn't done to show fear to the natives."*

THEME QUESTIONS

- Research the British Empire and its colonies. How powerful was it and how far did it extend? Examine such issues as its treatment of native peoples and its use and abuse of power.
- What group(s) do you think suffered most in the clash of the two powers in this text?
- Describe one incident that clearly shows the guards abuse of power in Belalau.
- Chart the changing power relationship between Bridie and Sheila through the text. You may wish to use a diagram for this response.

Relationships

The central relationship in the play is the one between Bridie and Sheila but there are other relationships that illuminate issues in the play. Some examples of these are

- Sheila's mother/ Sheila
- Rick/Bridie
- Rick/Sheila
- Lipstick Larry/Sheila
- Bridie's dad/Bridie
- Bridie/Barnie
- Bridie and Sheila/other survivors

Other examples can be found but these are the main relationships Misto uses to examine his thematic concerns. For example Sheila's selfless act of selling herself to Lipstick Larry is made more poignant when we understand her upbringing and relationship with her mother.

Her traditional English/British upbringing has made her decision all the harder and her 'properness' or propriety has stayed with her all her life. When she meets Bridie again she is wearing gloves,

> *"It's the sign of a lady. Mother always used to say that. She wore her best pair into Changi."*

This image and distinctively visual portrayal of ladylike behaviour did not help her in the camps and she had to change to survive. Aspects of her mother still cling to Sheila years later.

Sheila's relationship with Lipstick Larry was forced on her and it was the result of the power he had over life and death. We have already examined how power corrupts and Larry uses this to force a purely sexual relationship on Sheila, which scars her for life.

> *"Every night when I fall asleep, Lipstick Larry's waiting. He calls to me and I go to him – and no one can change that. Not even you."*

This description of Sheila's post traumatic stress is conveyed through the visual imagery of nightmare. The superlative, "every" combined with the ominous verb "waitinq" and the powerful "calls" serve to heighten the ongoing horror of the war.

It is heroism, however, along with shared experienced that bind relationships, especially in times of adversity such as war. Other women also show heroism in the play and Misto makes us realise that it is not only men who bravely risk their lives for others.

Yet, it is the close relationship between Bridie and Sheila that is the main focus. From the start when Bridie saves Sheila from drowning until their release at the end of the war they are inseparable. Despite what they have to deal with during the war they remain strong together. This bond helps them reconcile their relationship in the end.

During the reunion they have to deal with much pain and some recrimination. They come together again, however, and to some extent they are also reconciled with the wider community through their ability to tell the truth.

> "And that's when I realised I had to talk about it. There are probably thousands of survivors like us – still trapped in the war – too ashamed to tell anyone. Lots of people will be watching when Rick's programme goes to air. It mightn't be too late to – "

The telling of the truth in the visual, public arena is possibly their biggest act of heroism and it allows other women in the same situation the chance to do the same. The fact lots will be "watching" conveys a sense of the distinctively visual with regard to the medium and the public arena and thus, heightens the theme of truth and its centrality.

Relationships are extremely important in the play and Misto uses them to show not only how people are interdependent but how these relationships can have a profound effect on an individual's life and psychology. Many of these key points are conveyed with reference to the distinctively visual either in form, imagery or literal image.

Theme Quote

> *"Bridie Cartwright was the best – the best nurse – the best thief – the best woman in our camp. And I'd do it all again if I had to!"*

THEME QUESTIONS

- How does Sheila's mother influence her life? Do you think this has been a positive or negative influence? Support your response with direct quotes from the text.
- What influence does Bridie's father have on her?
- Describe what you know of Bridie's relationship with her husband, Barnie, from your reading of the text. Find one quote that shows how she feels about him even after his death.
- How does Sheila's relationship with Lipstick Larry affect her?
- Describe how Bridie and Sheila become reconciled.

War

The concept of the play is based around what happened to the two women during the war years from 1942 to 1945. Misto doesn't become too didactic about the war but lets the events speak for themselves. The atrocities of the war are clearly shown in the treatment of the prisoners. War seems to provide an excuse for people to act abominably toward others and this is felt for years afterward.

War seems to remove all moral concerns and common sense. For example when the British heard

"that the Japs had been raping army nurses"

they planned to shoot their own nurses to stop this happening. The Japanese stand condemned in the play before the camps. They attacked civilian ships with women and children aboard.

"Some Japanese Zeros found us. They dropped twenty-eight bombs on the Vyner Brooke...Then the Japs strafed the decks and shot up the life boats."

It is the behaviour in the camps that is the most horrifying. Even if the Japanese attitude to prisoners is taken into account, the policy of brutality and starvation is one of the horrors of the war.

"The first few weeks were a nightmare. Women sobbing for their husbands. Babies crying – always hungry. And the Japs'd come around and beat us for the fun of it. 'Useless Mouths' they used to call to us."

Conditions just got worse through the course of the war and thousands died, especially after the Japanese introduced their kill all prisoners policy.

It is interesting that no one seemed to understand the atrocities the women faced in the camps. The message from Curtin sums it up clearly,

"I have good news for Australian womens. Your Emperor, Mr Curtin, sends his greetings. And orders you all to keep smiling."

The inane and ludicrous nature of this message shows how ignorant governments were and as the war ended the Japanese became more vicious.

"For them it was business as usual – starving us, bashing us, withholding the quinine. And more and more women perished every day."

While the war is condemned Misto points out that it does produce some good. The courage of the women is never questioned in the face of extreme brutality. Both individuals like the 'bedpan nurse' and groups such as the choir show amazing resilience in the face of the horrors of war.

We also see relationships develop and flourish against all odds. Bridie and Sheila, for example, support each other and this support enables them to survive. This survival may be a scarred one but they are able to survive and eventually move on.

It is useful to note that the authorities and governments try to keep what the women suffered in war a secret. Even photos of their condition were not taken

"There aren't any photos of us, remember. Your army wouldn't allow them until we'd all fattened up a bit." Again, this represents cover up through the absence of the visual.

In *The Shoe-Horn Sonata* war is shown to be what it is – horrific and destructive both physically and psychologically. The only positives are the relationships and bravery the women show in their determination to survive.

Theme Quote

"Grave-digging mostly. We'd be too weak to stand—let alone use a hoe—so we'd get down on all fours, four graves a day were required."

THEME QUESTIONS

- Describe two incidents in the text and show how Misto uses them to criticise war.
- Amidst the horror there are some incidents of humour. Examine one of these incidents and discuss how it is humorous in the context of the war and also in the play.

Some incidents you may consider are

- Lipstick Larry and the pin
- The Japanese Brass Band
- Christmas Carols by the male POWs
- John Curtin's message
- Describe one positive thing to come from the war.
- Why does Misto highlight the cruelty of the Japanese prison guards?

DRAMATIC TECHNIQUES

The staging of *The Shoe-Horn Sonata* would physically seem to be quite straightforward. At the most two actors are on stage at any one time and the backdrop is a screen which shows the images which are integral to the production. These images, combined with particular music, tend to close the episodic scenes in the play and add another visual layer.

It is important to remember that these images are a key element of the play. Misto makes this clear in his detailed instructions. Combining music, image, light and sound helps to convey meaning. The visual images show exactly what the women are talking about and add to the sense of theatre.

- Make a list of the images shown in the text. Choose three of these images and place them in their context in the play. Describe how they add to the overall impact of the play and how they would affect the audience. This is a valuable exercise in relation to the elective.

The sounds that Misto suggests are also important, as is the music. These link both to the action and memory of the two women. The songs delineate the theme or idea being conveyed in the scene and touch an element of the dialogue. Each song has a particular meaning and these are worth investigating. Also remember the title of the play suggests a musical intent.

- Go to the music listed earlier in the book. Find one or two examples and listen to them. Compose a short analysis of one hundred words on each saying how they impact on the play. Remember that song lyrics can be found on the internet.

It is not only the music that Misto uses but sounds as well to help establish the mood for the audience and add to the theatrics of the play. For example when the two women are talking about the evacuation of Singapore we hear,

> *'Sound: the distant sound of lapping waves as SHEILA continues to speak.'*

At other times we hear the sounds of a young Sheila, young Bridie and the sound of machine gun fire. Each sound has a specific purpose to enhance an incident being portrayed.

- Make a list of the sounds in the play. Choose two and discuss how they enhance the message the dialogue and action is conveying.

As well as the focus on sound the use of silence is important and it is used to emphasise a moment of tension or indecision. The play itself begins with darkness and silence.

> *'Darkness. Out of the silence comes the voice of BRIDIE'*

The use of silence continues throughout the play at various stages. It is also important to note that Misto indicates when he wants silence in the script. This is not open to directorial interference and highlights how important it is to the overall impression that the playwright wishes to create.

Once the silence stops the dialogue begins and here Misto uses mainly a colloquial tone suited to oral history. For, this is what we are getting – oral histories of aspects of war and the relationship between Sheila and Bridie.

- How does Misto use silence? Explain how effective you think it is in the context of the play.

The use of the Japanese words such a "Keirii", "Ichi", "San" and "Ya-ta" give an air of authenticity to the play and the women's story as it shows that they have first hand experience of the culture. Misto also uses humour to break the tension of the play. Even though it deals with a serious subject, *The Shoe-Horn Sonata* has some very funny moments and the women use this laughter to survive some tough times.

- Examine the use of humour in the text by analysing one incident in detail.

Part of Misto's success in *The Shoe-Horn Sonata* is the dialogue between the two characters that gives them an instant relationship in the second scene. The personal comments and bickering, the links to the past and banter can only have come from knowing someone well. Their unified stance at the end of that scene indicates their unity but not reconciliation, that is to come.

- How do we know that the two women have been close? Find a specific example to support your answer.
- How do we know that Bridie is Australian?
- Sheila is British but she speaks in an Australian idiom. Explain.

To complete a basic analysis of the language techniques also examine the use of the shoe-horn as a symbol. A symbol is an object that represents something more and the shoe-horn grows in importance as the play progresses. At the beginning it is an object used to put shoes on but in the end it is far more and indeed, it is the last thing an audience sees.

- Compile a list of when the shoe-horn is seen or mentioned in the play. Discuss how the shoe-horn is used to parallel the events that the women are swept up in.

- Are there other symbols in the play that you can identify? The concept of the sonata is one you may consider.

- How are music, silence, dialogue and symbol all used to give greater depth to a portrayal of character?

- How effective is the distinctively visual in conveying themes and concepts in this play?

- How do written, spoken and visual languages combine in this play to present a clear, distinctively visual picture of War?

- How do written, spoken and visual language reveal how language can shape relationships and change perceptions of people and the world? Refer closely to your prescribed text and one related text.

ESSAY

Read the question below carefully and then examine the essay outline on the following pages. Try to develop your essay along these lines. Also develop strategies to answer questions that are not essay based.

A list of these response types is given at the end of the sample essay. Look at these and you should be familiar with most of them. Try to practise them when you can. Develop your writing skills.

QUESTION

How do the distinctively visual elements of the play impact on the play as a whole and on the intended audience?

- Discuss this statement with reference to *The Shoe-Horn Sonata*.

THE ESSAY FORM

The essay has been the subject of numerous texts and you should have the basic form well in hand. Ensure you link the paragraphs both to each other and back to your argument (which should directly respond to the question). Also, ensure your argument is logical and sustained with textual evidence.

Make sure you use specific examples and that your quotes are accurate. To ensure that you respond to the question make sure you plan carefully and are sure what relevant point each paragraph is making. It is solid technique to use topic sentences and actually 'tie up' each point by explicitly coming back to the question.

When composing an essay the basic structure is an Introduction, Main Body and Conclusion.

As well as this basic structure you will need to focus on:

Audience – for the essay the audience must be considered formal unless specifically stated otherwise. Therefore, your language must reflect the audience. This gives you the opportunity to use the jargon and vocabulary that you have learnt in English. Ensure your introduction is clear and has impact. Avoid slang or colloquial language including contractions (like doesn't, eg, etc.).

Purpose – the purpose of the essay is to answer the question given. The examiner evaluates how well you can make an argument and understand the module's issues and its text(s). An essay is solidly structured so its composer can analyse ideas. This is where you earn marks. It does not retell the story or state the obvious.

Communication – Take a few minutes to plan the essay. If you rush into your answer it is almost certain you will not make the most of the brief 40 minutes to show all you know about the question. More likely you will include irrelevant details that do not gain you marks but waste your precious time. Remember an essay is formal so do not do the following: story-tell, list and number points, misquote, use slang or colloquial language, be vague, use non sentences or fail to address the question.

ESSAY – THE SHOE-HORN SONATA

How do the distinctively visual elements of the play impact on the play as a whole and on the intended audience?

Discuss this statement with reference to *The Shoe-Horn Sonata.*

A few notes about the question:

- Remember the actual question is asking you what you have learned about the **effect** of the distinctively visual – in the play. Mention techniques and their effects.

- The question is to point you in the right direction but you must define the terms carefully. In this module you are usually required to respond with related material as well as the set text.

- It is important you take note of the ideas the question raises and check your response does address them. In other words ANSWER THE QUESTION!

- Take care you examine the play closely. This module is Distinctively Visual and you are required to form an understanding of the play with this in mind.

- You MUST have quotations and textual references that show you have a good knowledge and understanding of your prescribed text and the other related material that you use.

PLAN: Don't even think about starting without one!

Introduce...

the play, characters and examples you are using in the response

Definition:

explanation of how the play presents the visual elements

- Argument: that the visual elements are distinctive but they do impact the play and audience

You need to let the marker know what text you are discussing. It is good to start with your definition but it could have come in the first paragraph of the body. You MUST state your argument in response to the question and the points you will cover as part of it. Don't wait until the end of the response to give it!

Idea 1 – impact on the play

- explain the idea
- where and how shown
- Here you will give specific examples and show how subject matter and technique affect the play
- Perhaps one example of related material here

Idea 2 – impact on audience

- explain the idea
- where and how shown
- Here you will give specific examples and show how subject matter and technique affect the audience
- Perhaps one example of related material here

You can use the things you have learned to organise the essay.

Two ideas are usually enough as you can explore them in detail.

- Summary of two key ideas
- Final sentence that restates your argument

Make sure your conclusion restates your argument. It does not have to be too long.

© Five Senses Education Pty Ltd

ESSAY OUTLINE

How do the distinctively visual elements of the play impact on the play as a whole and the intended audience?

- Discuss this statement in reference to *The Shoe-Horn Sonata.*

Miso's play *The Shoe-Horn Sonata* incorporates distinctively visual elements such as photographic backdrops, costuming, proxemics, the show within a show concept and, through language, strong imagery including symbolism as well as tone, to convey the story of two female POW's and the atrocities they endured in WWII. Such concrete and linguistic "visual" representations convey images which, when combined with auditory aspects such as music, dialogue and silences, reveal the atrocities, humiliations and power games that make up aspects of war and the previously unseen experiences of many like Bridie and Sheila. Thus, the visual elements serve to strengthen the emotive aspects of the theme and heighten the message of the horror of war.

Now, you complete the main body and conclusion. If you are having trouble, ask your teacher to help you shape topic sentences for the main body and conclusion.

The content for this essay has been covered in the different relevant sections of the study guide and you have a clear guideline and plan. What you need to do in response to this question is to focus on getting your knowledge across to the marker.

Always relate examples to the question, the elective and the module and show how the techniques of the composer affect the text and the intended audience. Here it is important that you use the right terminology and the language of English specific to that form. Regarding this text, you really need to know and use the language of visual literacy and the language of drama / theatre.

Don't forget, in the introduction, to not only set your thesis (answer the question) but also introduce your related material and discuss briefly how it relates to the module.

OTHER TYPES OF RESPONSES

It is crucial students realise that their responses in the examination, class and assessment tasks will NOT necessarily be essays. This page is designed to give guidance with the different types of responses which may be required.

The response types covered in the exam may include some of the following:

- Writing in a role
- Journal/Diary Entry
- Brochure
- Point of view
- Radio interview
- Television interview
- Letter
- Feature article
- Speech
- Report
- Obituary
- Essay

Students should familiarise themselves with these types of responses and be able to write effectively in them. You should practise each one at some stage of your HSC year.

For a comprehensive explanation of each of these writing forms see:

Pattinson, Bruce and Suzan, *Success in HSC Standard English: A Practical Guide for Senior Students*

RADIO INTERVIEW

This work uses a suitable register but is far too general. Annotate this response, making reference to specific examples linked to your elective, The Distinctively Visual.

Song fades into station theme

Announcer: Welcome listeners to Meet The Playwright our regular 3pm Sunday feature here on 3XXX, the station for the Arts. I'm Tristan Kerboplle and today we welcome John Misto, writer of several television documentaries and mini-series as well as a number of plays especially the well-known *Shoe-Horn Sonata*.

Today we will be discussing this thought provoking play. John, welcome. It's a pleasure to have you in the studio today to discuss *The Shoe-Horn Sonata* since it has won several awards. How do you feel about awards John?

Misto: Good afternoon listeners and Tristan. Thanks for that introduction. Awards...well they do recognise achievement to a degree. I guess they show the play still has relevance after it is written and not just to the playwright. I wanted my play to come alive to a new audience who had not necessarily lived through the experience of war. The first production is always nerve wracking. No matter how confident you are the audience's reaction is vital.

Announcer: Yes, well, (laughs) The audience reaction seemed very positive! I saw the premiere at the Ensemble Theatre and it was a standing ovation.

Misto: That was great! The audience reacted to the emotion of the characters' experience in the camps and their triumph over adversity. I think that the concept of friendship is universal, as is the trauma of war on the human psyche. Audiences recognise the bond of friendship between the nurses, especially Bridie and Sheila and relate to the memories if not the exact experience. You saw the play and that is key – it is difficult for students studying it if they cannot visualise the characters and see the projected images.

Announcer: Well that's a good point. Although you say the idea of memory is important to the plot of the play. Students can grasp this from the script alone can't they?

Misto: Yes but I devised the TV documentary to facilitate this.(Explain further)

Announcer: Was this based on your own TV experience?

Misto: Definitely – yes...it did come from my Television work, Tristan, but the idea of memory came from talking to the surviving nurses from the POW camps. Bridie and Sheila are a combination of many experiences. Memory is important and I don't want their suffering to be simply forgotten. Contemporary audiences appreciate this.

Announcer: These experiences are indeed unique and you emphasis this by the use of songs and music. You use songs through the play. Let's give the listeners an example. *Plays the 'Rice Song' to the tune of Grangers Country Garden.* Why did you use this modern technique?

Misto: Well the nurses found them integral to the experience. Multimedia is a very contemporary thing and audiences use it to focus. I try to recreate the feeling of the situation through song. I am very specific in my stage directions, down to giving detailed description on tone and delivery. For example, I write instructions like "politely but with effort" at one point to show the strain between characters. Modern audiences detect this quickly and it makes it more... emotive. Relationships are universal and remain relevant. In this way the past and present can be interwoven.

Announcer: Songs, Dialogue – do you think this might have worked as a radio play?

Misto: oh no—while I can create pictures for the audience through the words and sounds, the costuming, lighting, stage positions are vitally important. I also use photographs to represent the past. (For example...)

Announcer: Hmmm...I have read that it is this idea of the past affecting the future in a profound way will keep the play relevant for contemporary audiences. How do you feel about that statement?

John: I hope it's accurate, but it is hard to judge your own work in this way. I mean only time will tell.

Announcer: You're right. Thanks for that John. We are about at the end of our time and I'd like to play another song from the play. Do you have a favourite?

John: The listeners may enjoy 'I'll Never Walk Alone'.

Announcer: Very apt for the nurses. (Explain) Aqain, thank you John. Here is 'I'll Never Walk Alone' on 3XXX. After the song stay tuned for our Renaissance Literature Hour.

Song has faded in and becomes louder.

RELATED MATERIAL

Related texts can be similar or different. You may be looking to link to issues or themes in your prescribed text such as courage, loyalty, war and the brutality of conflict, prejudice—racism, the impact of memory and friendship. These can all affect perspectives; ways of viewing the world and others. Consider also the purpose of writing. John Misto states his purpose in writing *The Shoe Horn Sonata* in the preface of the play.

"There is no national memorial to the many Australian nurses who perished in the war. At the time this play was first performed, the government had rejected all requests for one in Canberra. I do not have the power to build a memorial. So I wrote a play instead."

Film

The Railway Man (2013)

Eric Lomax (Colin Firth), a British POW, discovers that the Japanese interpreter who tortured him is still alive. He and his new wife (Nicole Kidman) confront the man.

Directed by Jonathan Teplitzky, this film is based on a story by Eric Lomax, *The Railway Man: A POW's Searing Account of War, Brutality and Forgiveness*. The filmic images may work to complement the visual images presented in the play. Like the text, it presents the brutality of conflict and the power of resolution.

Paradise Road (1997)

A war film that tells the story of a group of women, imprisoned by the Japanese in Sumatra during World War II. It was directed by Bruce Beresford and stars Glenn Close. In many ways, it is simiar to your prescribed text. Explore the ways the themes are presented visually through this different textual form.

The Pianist (2002)

Historical drama. Co-produced and directed by Roman Polanski, scripted by Ronald Harwood. It is based on the autobiographical book The Pianist, a World War II memoir by the Polish-Jewish pianist and composer Władysław Szpilman.

Poetry

Poets use words to create distinctively visual imagery in the audience's mind. Here you could look for descriptive poems about nature and natural elements. Explore how the poet has introduced new perspectives or ways of seeing or visualising something, through words. Poets always are trying to convey an idea or theme and the words have a purpose so they link well with the module and elective.

'THE ACTION IN THE GHETTO OF ROHATYN, MARCH 1942.'

by Alexander Kimel - Holocaust Survivor. This text highlights the power of memories.

Picture Books

These are a good source of visual imagery and any good library will have a variety for you to choose from. Try to choose one with a more sophisticated idea or concern so you can develop this as a link to the text. Here you will need to analyse the text using the language of visual literacy. Concept books on power, war or friendship might work well and provide a link.

Let the Celebrations Begin by Margaret Wild (Author), Julie Vivas (Illustrator). A story of hope, courage, friendship and liberation set in Belsen concentration camp. Recommended.

Memorial by Gary Crew and Shaun Tan http://www.shauntan. net/books/memorial.html#Memorial_comments. The link could be through memory and its impact.

The Island - Armin Greder, A picture book using a strong colour palette, contrasts and bleak images to deal with prejudice and discrimination.

Novel

The Pearl by John Steinbeck. A story of a pearl diver, Kino, a pearl, man's nature, greed and evil.

Art

Art and photography are also sources of related material and there are many artistic works, not just paintings, that are distinctively visual. This is another area you could explore. Eg Nick Ut's Napalm Girl.

ADDITIONAL QUESTIONS

1. An expert on theatre is writing a feature article for Drama World magazine to celebrate Misto's play *The Shoe-Horn Sonata*. The article argues that Misto's play has distinctively visual features that make it a valuable play in Australian theatre history.

   Write the article referring to specific incidents in the play *The Shoe-Horn Sonata*.

2. 'Misto's work is more about people than events.'

3. To what extent do you agree with this statement? In your answer refer specifically to the prescribed text *The Shoe-Horn Sonata* and incorporate aspects of the rubric.

4. 'Misto is celebrated for both his important messages and the effective language techniques he uses to represent them.'

   From your study of *The Shoe-Horn Sonata*, would you agree with this statement?

5. Imagine you are John Misto. Write a series of journal entries where you reflect on the success of *The Shoe-Horn Sonata*. You need to discuss intended messages and the techniques used to convey these ideas.

6. Two HSC students studying Misto are discussing the value of *The Shoe-Horn Sonata*. Write their conversation. They speak about their responses to the play's ideas and techniques and its relevance to the elective.

7. Create a visual representation of your response to *The*

Shoehorn Sonata. Your representation should include relevant graphics, key words and phrases and anything else you feel communicates your response. When complete, write a reflection statement where you explain your composition and how it represents your ideas about the play.

GLOSSARY OF TERMS

Allegro	Very fast. A musical term.
Andante	A musical term that means moderately slow.
Bamboo	A tropical treelike grass that has hard wood stems that are hollow.
Barrage	Artillery fire that comes in large amounts designed to destroy everything. A barrage can be verbal eg one person yelling at another.
Bayonet	Object like a knife attached to the front of a rifle. Used to stab or cut the enemy.
Bliss	A feeling of complete happiness.
Brooch	A piece of jewellery that is attached to a dress by a pin.
Brothel	A place or building where prostitutes entertain clients for money.
Cerebral	Anything relating to the brain.
Charcoal	The black substance left after burning wood.
Choir	A group of singers that are organised to sing particular songs.
Chooks	Australian colloquial term for chickens.
Conga line	A dance where a group form a line and dance.
Coo-ee	Australian term for a call when saying hello or looking for someone.
Decadent	Refers to an individual falling into moral decay.
Edible	Anything that is fit and able to be eaten as food.
Emaciated	Person made to be very thin by lack of food and/or disease.
Evacuate	To move away from a place of threat, danger or disaster. Usually refers to large groups.

Fag	Slang term for cigarette
Ferry	A boat used to move passengers from one place to another.
Fever	Usually associated with a rise in body temperature. Fevers are one part of a disease, some of which can lead to death.
Flustered	To become excited and confused.
Haggard	To look thin because of worries, ill health or over work.
Humiliate	To embarrass a person and take away their pride.
Hymn	A song sung in honour of God. Usually sung as a form of praise.
Impoverished	To make someone poor.
Kow tow	A stiff bow from the waist in Japanese culture that is used to show respect.
Lecture	A talk on a subject given to an audience.
Liberate	To make free. Eg. We are going to liberate the prisoners.
Lice	The plural word for a small, wingless blood sucking insect that infests people.
Loin-cloth	It is a piece of cloth worn on the hips to hide the genitals and bottom. Like underpants.
Malaria	A disease passed to people by mosquitoes that causes fevers and can kill.
Mature	Fully developed in both mind and body.
Menstruation	The monthly act of discharging blood from the woman's uterus.
Missionary	A person who goes to another country to tell people about his/her religion.

Mug shot	A photograph of a person's head taken by the police for their records.
Myopic	Near sightedness.
Nips	Slang term for the Japanese, often used in a derogatory way.
Orchestra	A group of players with different musical instruments that perform music.
P.O.W.	Abbreviated version of Prisoner of War.
Passed away	A common term used to describe someone who has died.
Patriot	A person who loves their country and supports it to the full at all times. In the play Sheila is described as a patriot.
Pier	A long platform, usually of wood, built over water to allow people to get on and off boats
Porter	A person employed to carry luggage or loads. In the war prisoners did this for food.
Prestissimo	A musical term for the most rapid tempo
Quinine	A medicine used to treat malaria.
Racist	A person who thinks that one race or type of people is better than another.
Rape	To have sexual intercourse with an individual against their will. Usually with force.
Red Cross	Organisation that, as one of its jobs, tries to ensure prisoners are treated well.
Red light district	Term used to describe a street or area where there are prostitutes and brothels.
Risotto	An Italian rice dish.
Saki	Japanese alcoholic rice wine drunk with meals.

Shoe-horn	It is a shaped piece of metal or horn that you place in the back of a shoe to make it easy to put on.
Snout	Part of an animal's head that refers, usually, to the nose and jaws.
Sober	Not drunk on alcohol.
Sonata	A long instrumental usually of three or four movements that tries to be balanced.
Squabble	A small argument.
Strafe	To attack with machine guns from an aeroplane. Eg. The Japanese flew past and strafed the ship.
Survivor	An individual who lives through a tough time.
Tribute	An offering to another person to show respect or gratitude. Can be money or written etc
Tuberculosis	A disease which is easily spread and infects the lungs. It eventually kills.
Waltz	A dance performed in ballrooms to a particular kind of music also called a waltz.
Whinging	Complaining.